cl🍀verleaf books™
Fall and Winter Holidays

Daniela's Day of the Dead

Lisa Bullard

illustrated by Holli Conger

M MILLBROOK PRESS · MINNEAPOLIS

For the Bengtson Family —L.B.
In celebration of all the ones I've lost —H.C.

Millbrook Press
A division of Lerner Publishing Group, Inc.
241 First Avenue North
Minneapolis, MN 55401 U.S.A.

Website address: www.lernerbooks.com

Main body text set in Slappy Inline 18/28.
Typeface provided by T26.

Library of Congress Cataloging-in-Publication Data

Bullard, Lisa.
     Daniela's day of the dead / by Lisa Bullard ; illustrated by
Holli Conger.
        p.   cm. — (Cloverleaf books—fall and winter holidays)
     Includes index.
     ISBN 978-0-7613-5084-2 (lib. bdg. : alk. paper)
     1. All Souls' Day—Juvenile literature. 2. Mexico—Religious
life and customs—Juvenile literature. I. Conger, Holli ill. II. Title.
GT4995.A4B79 2013
394.266—dc23   2012000537

Manufactured in the United States of America
1 – PP – 7/15/12

TABLE OF CONTENTS

Chapter One
Waiting for Day of the Dead

Hi! I'm Daniela. I can't wait for **Day of the Dead**, my grandpa's favorite holiday.

Day of the Dead is called Día de los Muertos in Mexico. It is also a holiday in parts of Central and South America.

UNITED STATES
OF AMERICA

MEXICO

SOUTH
AMERICA

N
W E
S

It's important in **Mexico.** My grandpa and grandma used to live there. Now my family lives in the United States. But we still celebrate this holiday.

For Day of the Dead, we **remember people** who have died. One of my school friends thinks it sounds sad.

In the United States, Day of the Dead is November 2. In Mexico, it often lasts for more than one day. There it might begin on October 31 or November 1.

But Grandpa always said it is a **happy time.**

Chapter Two

An Altar for Grandpa

This year, I'm **remembering** Grandpa.
He died a few months ago.

I really miss him. But Mama says Grandpa will be back to visit us on Day of the Dead! I won't see him, but I'll know he's here.

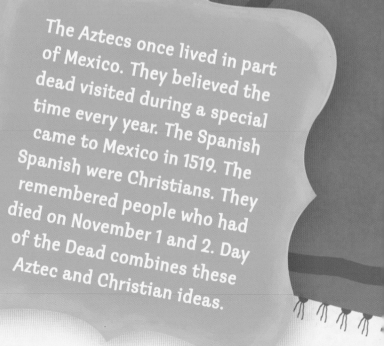

The Aztecs once lived in part of Mexico. They believed the dead visited during a special time every year. The Spanish came to Mexico in 1519. The Spanish were Christians. They remembered people who had died on November 1 and 2. Day of the Dead combines these Aztec and Christian ideas.

Mama's letting me help make our **ofrenda**, or **altar**. It's for Grandpa and other family and friends who have died.

That's where we put Day of the Dead things. Grandpa's picture helps us remember him.

He'll like seeing his favorite hat!

Some U.S. cities have public altars for Day of the Dead in schools or museums. Some cities also have parades, music, or dancing.

Chapter Three

At the Market

Mama and I pick out **sugar skulls** at the market. We also buy funny little **skeletons**.

Skeletons and skulls are common Day of the Dead decorations. They remind people of death. But they are not meant to be scary. Death is seen as just a part of life.

This skeleton is playing a **guitar** like Grandpa did.

13

We buy **bread of the dead** from the baker.

Sometimes there are bone shapes on bread of the dead. Sometimes little toy skeletons are baked inside.

I love it. **YUM!** But I'll be sure to leave lots for Grandpa on the altar. He loved it too.

Chapter Four

Celebrating!

On Day of the Dead, we visit the **cemetery.**
We clean Grandpa's grave.

Visiting graves also reflects both Aztec and Christian ideas. People might say Christian prayers for the dead. But they often bring marigolds. The Aztecs connected these flowers with death.

Miguel Fuentes

husband
father
grandfather

1938

We leave **marigolds** for him to smell. I'll put some on his altar too.

Lots of family members come to visit later. Everyone tells funny stories, especially about Grandpa.

I laugh until my belly aches. Or maybe that's because I ate too many **tamales!**

Aztecs ate tamales long ago. Many people think of them as a celebration food. They are cooked inside corn husks or leaves.

Day of the Dead is almost over. Then I'm going to keep Grandpa's hat in my room.

He'll look for it on the **altar** again next year!

21

Make a Macaroni Skeleton

Skeletons are seen everywhere for Day of the Dead. Now you can make your own skeleton out of pasta! There is a simple skeleton picture on this page for you to look at. But you may also want to find a larger picture of a skeleton. Look in a book or have an adult help you find one on a computer.

What you will need:

1 piece of black construction paper
A white crayon
Glue that dries clear

A wide variety of dried pasta (try to have as many different shapes available as possible)

Make your skeleton:

1) Using the white crayon, draw a stick figure on the black paper.

2) Study the skeleton picture. Notice the different parts of the body: arms, legs, and skull.

3) Now look at the different kinds of pasta you have. Which kind would work best to make a round skull? Which kind would work best to make a long leg? When you decide which kind is best, set it on that part of your drawing.

4) Move the pasta around until you are happy with how your skeleton looks.

5) Glue the pasta onto your paper in the skeleton shape and let it dry.

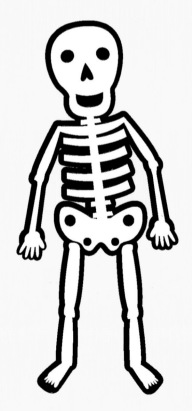

GLOSSARY

altar: a table or space to place religious items or, during Day of the Dead, items for and about dead people who are being remembered

Aztecs: a group of people who lived in part of Mexico hundreds of years ago

celebrate: do something to show how special or important a day is

cemetery: an area where dead bodies are buried

Christian: a person who follows the religion Christianity, which is based on the life and teachings of Jesus

decoration: things that are added to something to make it look special

Día de los Muertos (DEE-a day lohs MWEIR-tohs): "Day of the Dead" in Spanish

grave: the specific spot where a dead body is buried

husk: the outside covering of something, like the leaves covering corn ears

ofrenda (oh-FREHN-da): the Spanish word for "offering" and what Spanish-speaking people call a Day of the Dead altar

skeleton: the bones that support a human or animal body

skull: the bones that make up a human or animal head

tamales (tah-MAH-lays): food made from corn dough with a filling, such as meat, inside

BOOKS

Goldman, Judy. *Uncle Monarch and the Day of the Dead.* Honesdale: PA: Boyds Mills Press, 2008.
In this book, you can read a story about Lupita, who lives in Mexico and remembers her uncle on Day of the Dead.

Lowery, Linda. *Day of the Dead.* Minneapolis: Carolrhoda, 2004.
This book will help you learn more about the history and traditions of Day of the Dead.

McGee, Randel. *Paper Crafts for Day of the Dead.* Berkeley Heights, NJ: Enslow, 2008.
Find out how you can make many different Day of the Dead crafts.

WEBSITES

Maya & Miguel: **"La Calavera"**
http://pbskids.org/go/video/?category=Maya%20%26%20Miguel&pid=
ek8pghpt2JO1yDcQddR52XclDwFwIPFz
At this PBS Kids Go! website, you can watch an episode of the show *Maya & Miguel.* Maya does a great job on a school report about Mexico and Day of the Dead. But she also breaks her grandmother's sugar skull. What can she do to make things better?

Photos of Day of the Dead in Mexico
http://kids.nationalgeographic.com/kids/photos/gallery/day-of-the-dead/#
/day-of-the-dead-decorations_28133_600x450.jpg
See photos of toy skeletons, decorated graves, and ofrendas for a celebration of Day of the Dead in Mexico.